B55 003 764 3

D1178829

MA

2 0 MAY

0 9 JUL 2

This book m

The loan may
a further peri

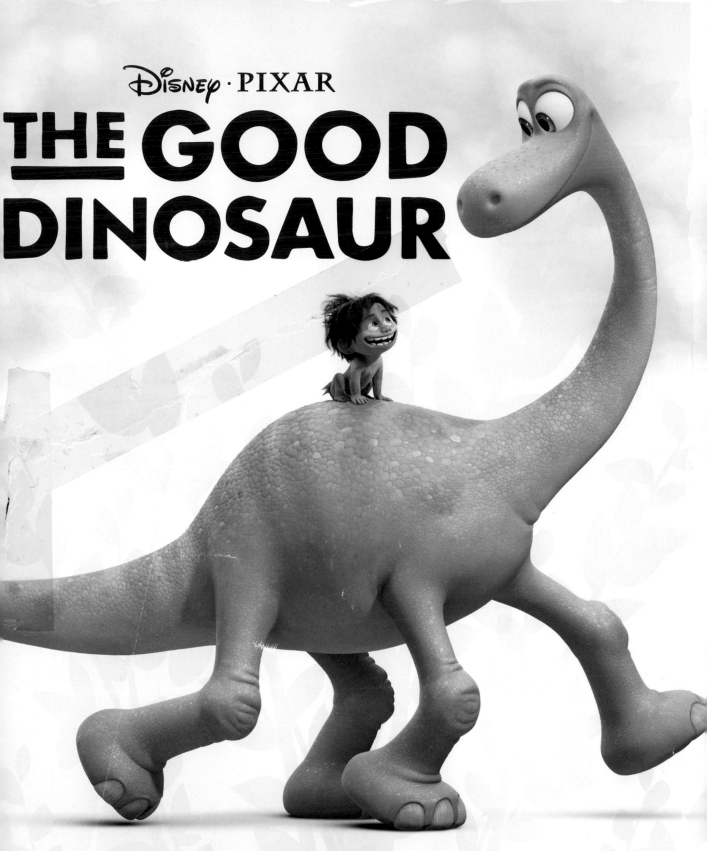

Disney · PIXAR

THE GOOD DINOSAUR

The Essential Guide

Disney · PIXAR
THE GOOD DINOSAUR
The Essential Guide

Written by Steve Bynghall

Contents

Introduction

On the prairies below Clawtooth Mountain, a family of Apatosauruses work hard on their farm, watering the crops and ploughing the fields. Little Arlo tries his very best to help out, but it's hard when there are so many scary things out there!

One day a raging river takes Arlo far away from home, and he must learn to survive in the wilderness. With a little help from some unexpected friends, Arlo can face the danger – and find the beauty – in the big wide world.

Arlo

Arlo is not your average Apatosaurus. The young dino is nervous about the big world around him. Despite being jumpy and jittery, Arlo does his best to fit in. He is friendly, fun-loving and always willing to help his family on the farm!

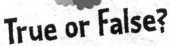

True or False?

Arlo has given names to some of the cluckers on the farm.

True! They include Henrietta and Eustice.

Shell-shocked

When Arlo hatches, his parents are surprised to find such a tiny dino inside a huge egg! However, his size doesn't matter – they love him just the way he is.

A strong will

Arlo might be a little timid but he has more than a little spirit. The young dino is determined to overcome his fears... but perhaps just not right at this moment!

Wobbly legs prone to stumbling

Friendly and warm smile

"I ain't a coward! And I'm gonna make my mark!"

Arlo

Clumsy claws

Arlo can be pretty clumsy – the gangly and awkward Apatosaurus is forever taking a tumble! It seems that Arlo can't do anything on the farm without tripping over or spilling something!

Outnumbered

Arlo feels safe with his family, but he still gets frightened easily. He even gets spooked by the flock of cluckers on the farm!

Did You Know?

Arlo is the youngest dino in the family by just a few seconds. He was the last egg to hatch, after his sister Libby, and his brother Buck.

Feet often used for running away from things

9

Poppa and Momma

Poppa and Momma work as a team – looking after their family, their farm and each other. The devoted dinos lead a peaceful and happy life, but it can be hard. Every harvest must be a success for the family to survive!

Poppa is the tallest in the family.

A strong bond

Arlo may get scared easily, but he knows that his Poppa will always protect him. Poppa does everything he can to help his son get over his fears and feel safe on the farm.

Did You Know?

Poppa and Momma's first names are actually Henry and Ida.

Poppa

Poppa shows great strength, both in his powerful body and in his determination to take care of his family. The resilient reptile remains focused and fearless, never giving up on anything – or anyone!

Powerful tail can clear a whole field.

"Sometimes you gotta get through your fear to see the beauty on the other side." Poppa

Ultra-long neck for ploughing

Momma

Warm-hearted Momma keeps the family going. Her love and good humour make every day feel better. However, it is her grit and spirit that allow the family to live at the farm year after year.

Passing on wisdom

Poppa and Momma keep a watchful eye on their children. The proud and patient parents teach their little ones everything they know about the world.

True or False?

Poppa and Momma got some T. rexes to build the farm.

False! They built it themselves.

Momma is skilled at seeding the fields.

The Homestead

Arlo's home sits peacefully below the spectacular three peaks of Clawtooth Mountain, and is a safe place for the family to work and play. Their house lies right next to fields of sown crops, as well as a river that runs all the way into the dangerous wilderness.

Jagged peaks of Clawtooth Mountain

Momma keeps a watchful eye.

Stone pit house with thatched roof

Neatly ploughed fields of corn

Expertly aimed
spray of water

Rain maker

To water the crops, Poppa takes
a mouthful of river water and
then sprays it through the gaps
between his teeth. Standing at
his full height, Poppa proves
that he's one skilled sprinkler!

Neck
stretched
up high

The unknown
wilderness
beyond...

Libby and Buck

Arlo's big brother and sister, Buck and Libby, work hard on the farm. They are eager to make their Momma and Poppa proud. But when they're not doing chores, they love joking around – especially when it involves teasing Arlo!

Did You Know?

Libby was the first egg to crack open. She is the oldest of the three siblings by about a minute.

A mischievous look on Libby's face

Long, graceful neck

Dark green stripes across Libby's back

Plougher power

When Libby's not playing, she's ploughing. She has turned out to be quite a fine farmer, and when it comes to ploughing she has real talent in the field.

Libby

Libby is always playing tricks – she loves hiding and then surprising her brothers. The looks on their faces never fail to make the playful prankster laugh.

"You mess up your chores, and everyone else's!" Buck

Log Lifter

From day one, Buck has been full of energy. The determined dino will go to great lengths to prove his strength, even lifting a whole tree with his teeth!

Buck and Libby's favourite pranks

Buck pretends he has been attacked by killer cluckers.

Libby sprays water all over her brothers.

Buck disguises his tail as a giant clucker.

Buck

Buck thinks it's cool to have fun, but he can be hot-headed sometimes. When Arlo messes up his chores, his big brother calls him a coward! Arlo is determined to prove him wrong.

Strong legs help Buck carry logs

Powerful tail for knocking down trees

Make Your M rk

On Arlo's farm, there is a special way of celebrating when a family member has achieved something great by working hard. On the corn silo, the determined dinos leave a muddy paw print to mark their success.

Buck

Buck earned his mark when he created a new field all by himself, knocking down and clearing out all the heavy trees. It was very tiring but also inspiring!

Libby

Libby earned her mark by ploughing an entire field on her own. She then succeeded in planting new seeds, exceeding everybody's expectations!

Momma

Momma built the entire house herself and also brought up the kids. That definitely deserves a mark on the silo – and a well-earned rest!

"You gotta earn your mark. By doing something big, for something bigger than yourself." Poppa

Arlo's mark

Every time Arlo sees his family's paw prints up on the silo, he longs to make his own mark. Unfortunately, his fears and his clumsiness mean that he's not so good at farm work. Earning his mark is going to be a challenge!

Silo made of stone holds corn

Family's paw prints made from mud

Poppa

Poppa's mark celebrates him building the silo! The silo helps to protect the corn from the harsh weather and thieving critters.

Fireflies

Poppa is determined to teach Arlo to be less frightened of what's around him, so they go on a night-time adventure! Poppa takes Arlo out to a dark field, and swishes his tail through the grass. Arlo is amazed when many fireflies suddenly fly into the sky, glowing brightly! A scary walk soon turns into a beautiful light show.

Long, lush grass in the field

Poppa's long tail swishing the fireflies

The bugs light up the night.

Arlo loves watching the beautiful lights.

Nose blow

When a firefly lands on Arlo's nose, he is completely spooked! However, when Poppa gently blows on the bug, Arlo sees the light. Fireflies are awesome, not alarming!

HOW TO:
CATCH A CRITTER

Poppa style

Poppa is furious when somebody steals corn from the silo! He sets Arlo the task of trapping the mysterious thief. Arlo finally has a chance to make his mark, but how exactly will he catch the critter?

1. Set a trap

Rope and net

Poppa builds a trap and shows Arlo how it works by raising the rope. When the critter grabs the corn on the ground, a net will fall and trap it!

2. Use a stick

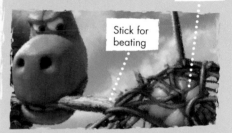

Pumpkin

Stick for beating

Poppa uses a pumpkin to show what happens when the trap is set off. A bell made out of nuts rings out. Then it's time to beat the critter with a stick!

3. Be brave!

Weights on the net

Poppa encourages Arlo to be brave. He's going to have to summon up all his courage when the critter is actually caught in the net!

1. Start worrying

Bell rings

When Arlo hears the trap go off, he freezes in terror. His brave moment has arrived but he feels more cowardly than courageous!

2. Do not panic

Nervous Arlo

It's time to beat the critter but rather than shaking his stick, Arlo starts to shake himself! The critter seems very angry so Arlo keeps a safe distance.

3. Set it free

Furious critter

When Arlo catches the critter's eye, he realises that he doesn't have the heart to harm another living creature. He lets the critter out of the net and it runs away!

HOW TO: CATCH A CRITTER
Arlo style

The trap has worked and the critter is captured! The time has come for Arlo to make Poppa proud… but will he be able to get past his fears?

Losing Poppa

When Poppa and Arlo tried to catch the critter, Poppa was tragically killed in a flash flood. Since then the family have felt very sad and struggle to keep the farm going.

Swept Away

One day, Arlo discovers the critter inside the silo stealing corn. Arlo blames the critter for what happened to Poppa, and chases him until they both tumble into the raging river! Arlo cannot swim, so he is soon swept under the water. He hits his head on a boulder and is knocked out!

"Momma! Momma!"
Arlo

Lost!

Arlo finally wakes up on the side of the river. He is shocked to find that he has ended up very far from home. Suddenly he hears a howl from the top of the cliff… it's the critter!

23

Spot

Human boy Spot is clever, courageous and an expert at surviving in the wild! Separated from his family early on, Spot has taught himself how to hunt, hide and build a shelter. He has also learnt to never give up!

True or False?

Spot is terrified of flying creatures called Pterodactyls.

True! They are one of the few things that he fears.

Super sniffer

Spot's time in the wild has given him an amazing sense of smell. His super-sensitive nose can follow a scent for miles. This is a gift that is not to be sniffed at!

Firefly fun

Curious Spot is never afraid of meeting new creatures. He is fascinated by the glowing fireflies and skilfully manages to capture one so that he can take a closer look.

"HoWWWWwWLLLLLLLLLLLLL!" Spot

Leaves in hair
for camouflage

Tree hugger

Spot has incredible
strength and agility.
Whether climbing trees
or swimming in rivers,
Spot is happy to go
almost anywhere!

A spot of company

Although Spot has grown
up on his own, the young
loner actually enjoys hanging out
with other creatures. In fact once you
gain his trust, Spot is a fiercely
loyal and lovable friend.

Strong arms
and legs for
running and
climbing

Did You Know?

Spot moves around on all
fours and can't speak the
way that Arlo can! Spot uses
grunts, growls and howls to
communicate with others.

Survival Test

It's pretty wild out in the wilderness and survival takes real skill. A rookie explorer like Arlo has a lot to learn, but for an adventurer like Spot, dodging danger is a real breeze. If Arlo wants to make it home again, he had better stay close to this critter!

Watch your step

If you stumble and tumble then watch where you land! A leg trapped between rocks could mean trouble. There's no getting out of such a tight spot.

Know your limits

If you're not tall enough to reach the berries on the tree, then you're just not going to reach them. Don't waste your efforts – you need a plan B to get food.

Take proper shelter

A strong storm demands an even stronger shelter – a pile of badly balanced branches just won't cut it! Take cover in a cave to stay dry.

Friend or enemy?

It's great to find a pal to help guide you around the wild, but how do you know if they are friend or foe? You must work out who you can trust and who you can't!

Work together

Two heads are better than one. Cooperating with each other, combining your skills and just having some company makes life in the wild a lot easier.

Look Fierce

If you find yourself cornered and your foe looks fierce, then look fierce back! If you manage to look more menacing than your enemy, then they might just back down!

Forrest Woodbush

Forrest Woodbush is one of the weirdest dinos in the wilderness! The strange Styracosaurus goes around the forest collecting pets. Forrest believes that each creature in his zany zoo helps to protect him from danger!

Critters of all shapes, sizes and colours.

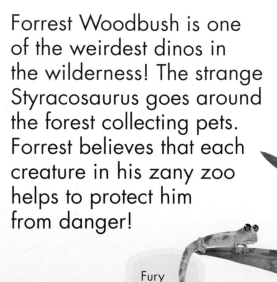

Fury

Destructor

Sturdy feet with very large toes

Woods watcher

Forrest likes to stay hidden in the trees and watch anyone who is passing. It makes him feel more mysterious! Arlo is shocked when Forrest suddenly appears!

Forrest's pets

Fury protects from creatures that crawl at night.

Destructor protects from annoying mosquitos.

Dreamcrusher protects from unrealistic goals.

"We've been watching you." Forrest Woodbush

Dreamcrusher

True or False?
Forrest's favourite critter in his collection is a red bird named Debbie.

True! But it's hard to keep her happy!

Peculiar perch
Each of Forrest's pets perches on one of his spiky horns. The oddball beast wants to add Spot to his mysterious menagerie, but will there really be room for one more?

Forrest fear
At first Arlo is scared of Forrest Woodbush. Forrest may not seem dangerous, but he comes out with the strangest sayings!

Beast

Funeral Planner

Hemorrhoid

Frank

Maniac

Violet

Lunatic

Name Game

When Arlo meets Forrest Woodbush, Spot hasn't even got a proper name yet. Arlo has only just stopped calling his companion a "critter"! Forrest challenges Arlo to a strange game to come up with a name for the human boy. If Forrest wins, he gets to add the boy to his pet collection!

Grubby

Cooty

Squirt

Stinky

Funky

Spike

Spot!

Spot on!

When Arlo shouts "Spot", the boy goes straight towards him. Arlo has won the game! Forrest tells Arlo that Spot will keep him safe on his journey home.

Becoming Friends

At first Arlo does not trust Spot. However, as the awkward adventurers spend more time together and help each other out, Arlo realises that they actually have a lot in common. They even have some fun and play games along the way! Could the peculiar pair end up as pals?

Howling pals

Both Arlo and Spot miss their families. As they howl into the night, the friends are glad that they at least have each other.

"OW—OOOOOOOOOO." Arlo and Spot

Gopher game

When Spot blows down a gopher hole, a gopher pops up into the air from another hole! Arlo joins in, and the pair are soon laughing as gophers start popping up everywhere!

Firefly Fun

Arlo shows Spot the breathtaking glow of the fireflies. Spot loves watching and playing with the spectacular insects just as much as Arlo does!

Thunderclap

Terrifying Pterodactyl Thunderclap leads a gang of winged scavengers. These fearless fliers believe that storms can provide anything – including food. They glide through the skies and swoop down to gobble up any wounded critters! Thunderclap will stop at nothing to catch his prey.

True or False?

Two of Thunderclaps's friends are called Sunnysky and Wispycloud.

False! He only hangs out with followers of the storm!

Meet and eat

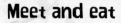

When Arlo first meets Thunderclap after a storm, the Pterodactyl seems friendly and helpful. However, the ruthless predator is only interested in eating Spot!

Thunderclap's gang

Downpour, Coldfront, Frostbite and Windgust are all named after the storm. They may belong to one gang, but when it comes to food, they fight each other for every last scrap!

Large
head crest

Wide
wingspan
for gliding

Sharp talons
for snatching
helpless critters

"The storm gave me a relevation and I wasn't scared anymore."
Thunderclap

Thunderclap's bizarre beliefs

The storm gave him his name.

The storm saved his life and made him brave.

The storm delivers tasty critter snacks to eat.

Storm Follower

Weather-obsessed Thunderclap believes that the storm has special powers. He thinks that it gave him a "relevation", which made him fearless.

Nash and Ramsey

From an early age, siblings Nash and Ramsey help their father, Butch, with herding longhorns. Growing up together has made them good friends, but there is still more than a little sibling rivalry!

True or False?

Nash has musical talent and plays the bug harmonica.

True! He loves to play it around the campfire.

Scare pair

Nash and Ramsey work together to leave their foes frozen with terror! They waste no time fighting off the Pterodactyls that attack Spot and Arlo.

Ultra-tough skin

Many scars from battles

Ramsey

Clever and quick-witted, Ramsey is as sharp as one of her claws! Very little rattles Ramsey – she loves the challenge of keeping longhorns in line.

Razor-sharp claws

"Nash! Boundaries! This is my personal bubble." Ramsey

Ramsey is focused and determined.

Nash is usually smiling.

Tender T. rex

Ramsey may act tough, but she does have a caring side, too. She keeps an eye on Arlo and reassures him things will be okay. She has an even softer spot for Spot!

Did You Know?

Nash loves to bother his big sister, especially with some T. rex wrestling!

Nash

Laid-back Nash isn't the brightest dinosaur out on the range. He spends most of his time daydreaming, when he should be keeping an eye on the longhorns!

Butch

T. rexes are the fiercest dinosaurs around – and Nash and Ramsey's father, Butch, is no exception! The tough-talking rancher might not be very touchy-feely, but Butch does have a softer side. If you can earn his respect and trust, you'll get a friend for life in return.

Doting Dad

Butch is proud of Nash and Ramsey. They help him herd the longhorns. By learning on the job they can follow in his (enormous) footsteps!

Did You Know?

Butch still has a croc tooth lodged in his jaw from a croc attack that happened many years ago!

Powerful tail can knock down foes.

Longhorn herder

Every day, Butch must round up his herd of longhorns and move them to new areas for grazing. It's lucky that Butch loves his job!

"If you're pullin' my leg, I'm gonna eat yours!" Butch

Old battle scar on jaw

Gruesome grin

Butch is a dino of few words and Arlo finds it hard to tell what he's thinking. Is that a gruesome grin or a frightening frown? With those teeth, it's just best to keep out of his way!

True or False?

Butch doesn't like talking about his adventures as a rancher.

False! He loves swapping stories with other dinos.

Veteran rancher

Butch is one of the best ranchers in the region. His years of experience, combined with his flair for scaring rustlers make him the last T. rex you should mess with!

Huge feet with sharp claws

39

Find the Herd

Butch and his family are trying to find their missing herd of longhorns. They suspect they might be at a waterhole, but the trail has gone cold. Suddenly Arlo has an amazing idea! Could Spot's super sense of smell catch the longhorn scent and find the hapless herd?

"Come on, Spot. Sniff it out, boy."

Arlo

Longhorn Life

Longhorns don't do much except munch grass! A longhorn stampede can be dangerous, but mostly they just move along to wherever the green stuff is.

Arlo is sure that his plan will work.

Arlo's deal

Arlo agrees to let Spot help the T. rexes. In return Butch agrees to take them to the waterhole, where there may be dinos who can help them get home!

Spot is already on the trail.

Losing the longhorns

Nash is anxious to locate the longhorns. The dopey dinosaur managed to lose them when he wasn't paying attention!

41

Raptor Pack

Raptors are some of the most despised dinosaurs around! These dim-witted fiends spend their time rustling longhorns and threatening prey. Raptors might be small, but when they attack together they are speedy, savage and seriously dangerous!

Did You Know?

Bubbha is the unofficial leader of the pack of raptors. The other three will do what he says!

Gang of thieves

Bubbha, Pervis, Earl and Lurleane are a really unpleasant pack. The fearsome four think nothing of stealing the T. rexes' herd of longhorns for themselves.

Earl is a very dim dino covered in dirty feathers.

Bubbha is the leader of the pack.

"I know you're there. I can smell ya!"
Lurleane

True or False?

Raptors would rather talk to other dinosaurs than fight them.

False! Raptors will fight anyone who gets in their way.

Cruel **Pervis** has very big teeth!

Lurleane always has a nasty look on her face.

43

Spot rocks!

Getting on top of a rock makes Arlo bolder than he's ever been before. When he screams, however, he loses his voice! Fortunately, a bite on the leg from Spot soon does the trick!

Unsettled longhorns start to stampede.

Daring duo

When Butch gets attacked by raptors, Arlo and Spot furiously rush to help. They headbutt a raptor right across the field!

44

HUFFLEPUFF

Get som

Battling Raptors

Butch is determined to defeat the rotten rustlin' raptors and hatches a plan! He asks Arlo to roar to attract the raptors, so that the T. rexes can then launch a surprise attack. The battle that follows is ferocious and frightening, so Arlo has to use all his courage to play his part!

Vicious raptors biting Butch

Arlo and Spot get mad and charge.

Raptor rout

Thanks to Arlo and Spot, the T. rexes triumph and the raptors are defeated! The dynamic dinos can carry on their journey with the herd of longhorns.

Nash

Nash got a scar on his foot by fighting off fifteen outlaw Steggos. One Steggo's spiky tail got stuck in Nash's foot and now he can't even feel his toes.

Butch

The huge scar on Butch's chin came from a croc bite. When some crocs launched a surprise attack from a waterhole, Butch got his revenge by biting one of them clean in half!

Battle Scars

T. rexes love telling tales around a roaring campfire, and showing off scars from their favourite fights. Their incredible stories help Arlo understand that he must learn how to get past his fears. That's when you find out what you're really made of.

Ramsey

Ramsey once got her tail stuck between a rock and a hard place just as a herd of longhorns was stampeding straight toward her. She had to chew the end of her tail off to escape!

Worried Arlo doesn't want Spot to leave.

Spot is amazed to see another human.

Return call

Spot and Arlo happily howl together, until they hear another howl in the distance. Could that be a human on the horizon?

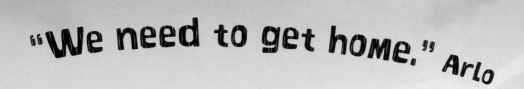

"We need to get home." Arlo

Distant human figure on the hillside.

Top of the World
As they reach higher ground, Arlo and Spot watch a spectacular sunset over Clawtooth Mountain. Their journey is almost over!

Best Buddies

Spot and Arlo say goodbye to the T. rexes and continue on their journey. As they get closer and closer to home, Arlo starts thinking about how much fun it will be having Spot living on the farm. He can't imagine life without his best friend around!

The Pterodactyls can't wait for their snack.

Circle and swoop

As the lightning flashes, Arlo and Spot see the Pterodactyls circling above. They swoop in for an attack, beating Arlo with their wings, and forcing him to the edge of a steep ridge.

Losing Spot

Arlo and Spot finally reach Clawtooth Mountain. However, before they can make it home, another storm hits – and the Pterodactyls return. Thunderclap and his crazy cronies see Spot as a tasty meal and are determined to snatch him away!

"No! Spot!" Arlo

Arlo is surrounded by the Pterodactyl gang.

Spot does his best to hold on to Arlo.

Thunderclap grips Spot in his talons.

Scratch and snatch

As Arlo is weakened by the gang's blows, Thunderclap grabs Spot! Arlo desperately tries to pull him back, but the Pterodactyl is too strong. Thunderclap flies away – taking Spot with him!

Arlo's Journey

Some journeys change you forever. Arlo's amazing adventure has turned the faint-hearted dino from cowardly to courageous. Arlo finally realises that his Poppa was right all along – he has much more fighting spirit in him than he ever could have imagined.

Nervous wreck

At the start of his adventure Arlo is easily frightened. The littlest things give him the jitters and the shivers. Arlo is one very panicky Apatosaurus!

Exposed to danger

As Arlo explores the wilderness, somehow things begin to seem a little less scary. Having a friend by his side makes it easier to be brave!

Getting braver

As Arlo realises that he is tough enough for adventure after all, he starts to show true guts! However, his fears still get the better of him sometimes.

"I knew you had it in you. Go take care of that critter." Poppa

Finding the courage

When Thunderclap takes Spot, Arlo is left trapped in thick brambles. Suddenly he sees a vision of Poppa, inspiring him to summon the courage to escape and save Spot. Arlo may be scared, but he knows that he can't leave his friend behind.

Trunk terror

Spot is trapped in a tree trunk! The Pterodactyls keep smashing into the wood to try and make Spot fall out, but he holds on for as long as he can.

Thunderclap closes in on Spot.

Windgust swoops in to attack Arlo.

The raging river water is rising.

Roaring rescue

A snarling Arlo uses all his strength to fight off the Pterodactyls. When Thunderclap attacks Spot once more, Arlo unleashes a furious roar and knocks him into the river!

"Well, look who got relevated." Thunderclap

Frostbite and Downpour will not back down without a fight.

Arlo Attacks

Arlo charges up the mountain and howls for Spot, until he hears his friend howl back. He finds Spot stuck in a tree trunk by the river, surrounded by squabbling Pterodactyls! As Arlo tries his best to rescue his buddy, a sudden flash flood threatens to sweep Spot and the tree away in a sheer wall of water.

No time to Lose

The flash flood is an epic force of nature, sweeping away everything in its path – including the tree Spot is in! Arlo bravely leaps into the water and swims to his friend.

Raging Waters

Arlo and Spot may have beaten off the Pterodactyls but they face an even greater danger. The flood washes them toward a waterfall! This is where the river – and everything in it – flows over a steep drop. Going over could mean the end for the terrified twosome!

Arlo and Spot are falling fast!

Raging river is impossible to escape.

Trees swept away by the flood

Steep drop

Arlo and Spot reach each other just before they are swept over the waterfall's edge! They hurtle down into the river below.

Branches carried over the falls

Safe on the shore

They made it! Arlo drags himself onto dry land and anxiously waits for Spot to open his eyes. When he does, Arlo is relieved to see that his friend is okay.

Force of Nature

The nature that surrounds Arlo has many sides. There is true beauty in the peaceful prairies and magnificent rivers. But there is also great danger in the dark forests and powerful storms. It takes real bravery to face everything that nature throws Arlo's way.

Peaceful peaks

From afar, the snowcapped peaks of Clawtooth Mountain Range look magnificent. They make the whole landscape feel calm and beautiful.

River of life

The river brings life to Arlo's family, as it helps their crops to grow. Following the river also helps Arlo find his way home.

Clear skies

On a cloudless night, the stars twinkle in the sky and the moon's reflection shimmers on the water. Everything is perfectly still and silent.

Mountain danger

Up in the mountains the rocky terrain is harsh and barren. The razor-edged ridges and sheer cliffs put even the most experienced climber on edge.

Flood of fear

When the river rises and the water rushes everywhere, there is no escape. The lethal currents of the flash flood sweep Poppa away.

A stormy night

In a violent storm, dark thunder clouds fill the sky and frightening lightning strikes the ground. Arlo must take shelter from the terrifying chaos!

A welcoming new family.

Arlo marks out a circle in the ground.

Goodbye Spot

Just as Arlo and Spot almost reach the farm, Spot is fascinated to meet another human family! He curiously approaches them and is happy when they greet him lovingly. When Arlo realises that Spot has a chance at joining a new family, he knows he must say farewell to his special friend.

Arlo is happy to see Spot get a new family.

Family circle

Arlo pushes Spot towards the family. He draws a circle to make a confused Spot understand that he should stay with the humans.

Hold on tight

Spot hugs Arlo tightly. The two friends have been through an amazing adventure together, which they will never forget.

Final howl

As Spot walks off with his new family, he glances back one last time at Arlo. Both boy and dinosaur let out a final howl to say goodbye.

Libby loves having Arlo back.

Buck sees his brother in a new light.

Arlo can't stop beaming.

Momma is overjoyed to see her son.

Confident Arlo

The family can see that Arlo's adventures have made him a stronger, more confident dinosaur. He even reminds Momma of Poppa!

Back Home

When Arlo returns to the farm, his family are amazed – they didn't know whether they would ever see him again! Arlo is the happiest dinosaur on the planet. It feels fantastic to be back home again, surrounded by his family.

Proud prints

Because Arlo showed so much bravery, he is finally allowed to display his paw print on the family silo. Arlo has made his mark at last!

Acknowledgements

Penguin
Random
House

Editor Lauren Nesworthy
Senior Designer Lynne Moulding
Pre-production Producer Siu Chan
Producer David Appleyard
Managing Editor Sadie Smith
Managing Art Editor Ron Stobbart
Publisher Julie Ferris
Art Director Lisa Lanzarini
Publishing Director Simon Beecroft

First published in Great Britain in 2015 by
Dorling Kindersley Limited
80 Strand, London WC2R 0RL
A Penguin Random House Company

15 16 17 18 19 10 9 8 7 6 5 4 3 2 1
001–193689–Oct/2015

Copyright © 2015 Disney Enterprises, Inc.
and Pixar Animation Studios.
All rights reserved.

All rights reserved. No part of this publication may be reproduced,
stored in a retrieval system, or transmitted in any form or by any means,
electronic, mechanical, photocopying, recording, or otherwise,
without prior written permission of the copyright owner.

A CIP catalogue record for this book
is available from the British Library.

ISBN 978-1-40933-845-1

Printed in Slovakia

Colour script paintings by Sharon Calahan

Colour script layouts by Erik Benson, Adam Campbell, Edgar Karapetyan,
Dean Kelly, Austin Madison, Kelsey Mann, J.P. Vine, Bill Presing,
Gleb Sanchez-Lobashov, Louise Smythe, and Rosana Sullivan.

Illustrations by Disney Storybook Artists

DK would like to thank: Chelsea Alon, Rima Simonian,
Stephanie Everett, Scott Tilley, Winnie Ho, Heather Knowles, Chuck
Wilson, Kelly Bonbright and Margherita Rosson at Disney Publishing,
and Victoria Taylor and Julia March for their editorial assistance.

A WORLD OF IDEAS:
SEE ALL THERE IS
TO KNOW

www.dk.com
www.disney.com
www.pixar.com